Rugby Made Simple

Ann Waterhouse

Rugby
Made Simple

An Entertaining Introduction to the Game
for Mums & Dads

Illustrations by Amanda Stiby Harris

Meyer & Meyer Sport

British Library Cataloguing in Publication Data
A catalogue record for this book is available from the British Library

Rugby Made Simple

Maidenhead: Meyer & Meyer Sport (UK) Ltd., 2015
ISBN 978-1-78255-063-1

Previously published as *Sue Porter's Guide to Rugby* in 2012 by Ann M Waterhouse Ltd.

© 2015 by Meyer & Meyer Sport (UK) Ltd.
Aachen, Auckland, Beirut, Cairo, Cape Town, Dubai, Hägendorf, Hong Kong, Indianapolis, Manila, New Delhi, Singapore, Sydney, Teheran, Vienna

 Member of the World Sport Publishers' Association (WSPA)

Total production by: Print Consult GmbH, Germany, Munich
ISBN 978-1-78255-063-1
E-Mail: info@m-m-sports.com
www.m-m-sports.com

Dedication

This book is dedicated to that hardy band of supporters – mostly parents and grandparents – who brave all the appalling weather an average winter can throw at them to watch a bunch of grubby small boys or girls doing their best to kill each other each week (or so it seems to the uninitiated).

Contents

Acknowledgements

The author would like to thank:

Caterham School, whose myriad sporting activities inspired her to write the first edition of this book as a guide for its bewildered mothers.

The late Stephen Smith, former Headmaster of Caterham School and an England scrum-half, without whose early support this book would probably never have been published.

All the Caterham School sports masters from the latter part of the 20th Century, especially Pat Lavery and John Moulton, for their help and guidance in the preparation of the original books.

Her husband David, without whom her interest in the game would never have been kindled in the first place.

Gareth and Alan, for giving her a reason to stand on freezing cold touch lines for over 10 years, through every kind of wind and weather, and still enjoy every second of it.

And last, but not least, Amanda Stiby Harris for her imaginative, amusing and illuminating illustrations. The books would be very different without her input, and the author is extremely grateful for her inspiration and talent.

Amanda also helps with the text of the books, and for this guide her brother Robert also lent a hand checking our efforts to ensure accuracy throughout. I am so grateful to have had their support.

Introduction

Why write a series of books on sport for parents and others who never played the games themselves? I must have been asked that question so many times since the appearance of my first booklet on the game of rugby that was designed to inform and entertain the parents of Caterham School in Surrey, where my own two boys were enjoying multiple sporting activities in the guise of education.

There are, of course, many detailed books on the rules and techniques for playing this sport, but few of them are aimed specifically at the spectator, and none that I could find were aimed at parents or other relatives.

Any mother who has stood in the freezing cold on a rugby touch line will confirm that the more you learn about the game, the more enjoyable watching a match becomes.

So it was for me, and as my elder son's team was supported by parents with boys higher up the school whose knowledge was greater than mine, I was only too grateful for small crumbs of wisdom that they passed on to me during the course of school matches.

As the years progressed, I gradually felt I was beginning to understand this exciting sport, and in my turn I passed on some of my knowledge to the spectators watching my smaller son's matches. It was these good souls who kept saying, 'Why don't you write a book about it?' So it was all these experiences that inspired me to complete the books.

I will be explaining the game from a parent's point of view throughout this book, but the advice here applies equally to boyfriends and girlfriends, wives and husbands, and grandparents. Since the book was originally conceived with boys' parents in mind, I will generally use he, his and him, but please don't think this precludes the same information from applying to your young daughter if she's taken up the game at her local junior rugby club or school.

Indeed I can quote the Laws of Cricket as published by the MCC which state: 'The use, throughout the text, of pronouns indicating the male gender is purely for brevity. Except where specifically stated otherwise ... this book ... is to be read as applying to women and girls equally as to men and boys.' In other words, just because I don't say she or her doesn't mean that I'm not including the fairer sex too throughout the book.

Words in italics in this book refer to items listed in our glossary at the back of the book, so if you want a quick explanation of a particular term, just flick to the back pages, and you'll find it there.

Ann Waterhouse

What is rugby?

Origins and history

The game of rugby football, so history tells us, started in 1823 when a certain William Webb Ellis (a pupil at Rugby School) picked up a football and ran with it. After crossing the goal line, he reportedly turned to his sports master and asked, 'Is that a goal sir?' to which the master responded, 'No, but it's a jolly good try.'

This apocryphal tale has never been confirmed as fact, although this exchange is frequently quoted as the reason for a *try* being so named. However, it was some years later before the first official rules of the game were written down, again at Rugby School, in 1845.

After these rules were published, the game spread throughout England, and on 4 December 1870, Edwin Ash of Richmond and Benjamin Burns of Blackheath published a letter in *The Times* suggesting that 'those who play the Rugby-type game should meet to form a code of practice as various clubs play to rules which differ from others, which makes the game difficult to play.' On 26 January 1871, a meeting attended by representatives from 21 clubs was held in London at the Pall Mall Restaurant on Regent Street.

The 21 clubs present at the meeting were: Blackheath (represented by Burns and Frederick Stokes, the latter became the first captain of England), Richmond, Ravenscourt Park, West Kent, Marlborough Nomads, Wimbledon Hornets, Gipsies, Civil Service, The Law Club, Wellington College, Guy's Hospital, Flamingos, Clapham Rovers, Harlequin F.C., King's College Hospital, St Paul's, Queen's House, Lausanne, Addison, Mohicans and Belsize Park. The one notable omission was the Wasps. According to one version, a Wasps' representative was sent to attend the meeting, but owing to a misunderstanding, was sent to the wrong venue at the wrong time on the wrong day. Another version is that he went to a venue of the same name where, after consuming a number of drinks, he realised his mistake but was too drunk to make his way to the correct venue.

The game continued to develop until 1895, when a major dispute over payments to players led to the formation of a rival organisation, the Northern Rugby Football Union. These two organisations competed for control of the game, but neither truly succeeded. As a result, two forms of the game, or codes, developed. One was run by the Rugby Football Union and called Rugby Union; players of this code couldn't earn money from the game (although nowadays they can). The other was run by the Northern Rugby Football Union and was called Rugby League, and players of this code were paid to play.

The two codes have slightly different rules, with the most important differences being the way play is continued after a player has been tackled and the number of players on each team: 15 for Rugby Union and 13 for Rugby League.

Rugby Union at the top flight finally turned professional in 1995, just after the very first edition of this book was published, when the International Rugby Board (IRB), now branded as *World Rugby*, allowed payments to Union players for the first time in the game's history.

Players are now able to switch between the two codes without penalty over the course of their careers. World Rugby is the world governing and lawmaking body of Rugby Union. It is made up of 102 member unions and 18 associate member unions. Rugby is now played by men and women, boys and girls, in 120 countries by more than 7.23 million players. There are 2.6 million registered players, 4.63 million non-registered players, and of those over 1.8 million are female players. These figures date from 2014 and may well be even larger now. The World Rugby website will have the latest statistics if you really want to find out how much Rugby Union is growing across the world.

While the game of rugby originally developed from football, there are major differences between these two sports, apart from the most obvious one of being allowed to handle the ball in rugby. These also include the H-shaped goalposts and the oval-shaped ball. A rugby game is made up of two halves that last 40 minutes each, with a short interval at half-time. At junior level this is rarely more than 5 minutes, but at international level, it is usually 15 minutes.

You can find a detailed map of the world showing all the member nations, the year they joined World Rugby and their current player numbers in the latest annual review. Online here:

>> http://pulse-static-files.s3.amazonaws.com/worldrugby/photo/ 2015/03/05/61b7a966-a65a-4952-8b71-74bed89a8d7c/WR_2014_ Player_Numbers.jpg

The most recent addition to the rugby family is Costa Rica, which became an associate member in 2014.

To sum up the game, we quote the World Rugby website:

'Players are attracted to Rugby because of its unique character-building values.'

The 'sport is built upon the principles of camaraderie, fair play, respect and teamwork. Every player knows these principles are more important than winning or losing.

From the earliest steps in our sport, players are taught the basics of playing fair, enjoying the game and respecting the officials and opponents alike.'

The rugby World Cup

Many new supporters come to the game of rugby after watching televised international matches, such as the Northern Hemisphere's Six Nations annual competition or the World Cup. The latter competition was instigated in 1987 to bring together the leading rugby nations in a tournament that occurs every four years, timed to occur the year before the Olympic Games. Nowadays rugby playing nations from around the world compete in the early stages.

The first round for the finals is a pool stage. The format used since 2003 has 20 teams divided into four pools of five teams, with each pool playing a round-robin series of 10 games against the other teams in the same pool. Teams are awarded four points for a win, two points for a draw and none for a defeat. A team scoring four or more tries in one match will score a bonus point, as will a team that loses by seven points or fewer.

The teams finishing in the top two of each pool advance to the quarter finals. Then a further knock-out competition establishes who will get through to the final match. There are specialised websites telling you all about the Six Nations and the World Cup; if you'd like to learn more you can find the web links at the back of this book.

Scoring points

The main aim of rugby is to score points (not goals, as in football). This is done by the team carrying, passing and kicking the ball to the opposition's goal line and touching the ball down behind that line to score a try, worth five points.

This is then *converted* if a player can kick the ball over the crossbar between the goalposts, having previously placed it back on the *pitch* in line with the point where the try was scored. If the kick is successful, two more points are added to the score.

Alternatively, the ball can be kicked over the posts from either a *penalty kick* or a *drop kick* (kicking the ball after dropping it from your hands to bounce off the ground before kicking) in order to score three points. These are also described as penalty goals or drop goals.

For the past few years, the points scored from the various plays have remained the same, but over the years, the laws regarding scores have been changed on several occasions, so it's worth being aware that this may change at some point in the future, too.

Passing the ball away from the passage of play

Unlike most other sports, in rugby the ball must always be passed sideways or backwards (i.e. away from the passage of play and the opposition's *try line*). If the ball is passed forwards to a team colleague, this is called a *forward pass* and is penalised by the award of a *scrum*.

If the ball is dropped forwards, this is described as a *knock-on*, and if this action is considered to be unintentional, the referee will award a scrum to the opposition where the forward knock-on occurred. However, if the referee believes the knock-on or throw forward was intentional, a penalty kick is awarded instead, which could allow the opposition to score points immediately.

You can check out www.worldrugby.org/regulations for full details of the Laws of the game and detailed explanations of all the penalties that can apply in a game. This will give you a more comprehensive idea if you are interested in learning more. The Laws are game specific, too, with separate versions for U-19, seven-a-side and ten-a-side games.

The game was rightly proud of its five core values set up in the early 21st century. These were Integrity, Passion, Solidarity, Discipline and Respect. Every player – and indeed every supporter – should bear these five elements in mind when a game is taking place. They are key factors in every rugby game, wherever it is being played, and make the game what it is today, vibrant, exciting and fun to watch and play. Identified in 2009 by the World Rugby Member Unions, these were collectively known as World Rugby values and were incorporated in the Playing Charter – a guiding document that aims to preserve rugby's unique character and ethos both on and off the field of play.

They can be summed up as follows:

Respect: This covers respect for team-mates, opponents, match officials and all those involved in the game, and it is the paramount value.

Integrity: This is central to the fabric of the game; it is generated through honesty and fair play.

Passion: All rugby people have a passionate enthusiasm for the game, which generates excitement, emotional attachment and a sense of belonging to the global rugby family.

Solidarity: The game provides a unifying spirit that leads to lifelong friendships, teamwork, loyalty and camaraderie, which aims to transcend all cultural, geographic, political and religious differences.

Discipline: This forms an integral part of the game both on and off the field. It is reflected through adherence to the Laws, the regulations and to rugby's values.

These have been reduced now to Integrity and Discipline in the latest World Rugby information, but it's worth bearing in mind their origins.

There is obviously a great deal to learn about the basics of the game, but our starting point on the following pages is an explanation of the positions that players may have on the pitch and their roles within a game.

Playing positions

Rugby Union teams consist of 15 players, as opposed to a soccer football team of 11. School teams are often referred to as the First Fifteen, Second Fifteen, etc. (and this is sometimes written down using Latin numerals, XV). Each team is split almost equally between players known as *backs* and *forwards.*

The forwards are mainly responsible for getting the ball down the pitch towards the try line, using brute strength and techniques known as rucking, mauling and scrummaging, all of which we will explain in more detail later.

One of the most common forms of organised play for forwards, something you will see frequently during a match, is a type of group hug that seems like a team bonding exercise but is actually called a scrum (or *scrummage*).

The backs traditionally run with the ball in hand, passing it from player to player while running down the pitch until they are tackled by the opposition. If they are tackled and trip or fall over and are then held on the ground by a member of the opposition, or if they kneel down and are held, they must release the ball to the ground immediately. If they are able, they should attempt to pass the ball (ideally to a fellow team member) before they or the ball hit the ground.

However, if they land on the ground but manage to keep the ball off the ground, and they are not held firmly by an opponent, then they can stand up again and continue to run down the pitch towards the try line. This is called breaking a tackle. Backs pride themselves on being able to break several tackles in a row before they finally have to give up the ball. It's a very fine line between being tackled and having to release the ball and being halted and being able to continue.

In recent years, the differences in style of play between backs and forwards have been broken down, and now senior players have begun to adopt each other's playing techniques. It's not uncommon for forwards to join the back line in attacking the opposition, and backs nowadays frequently get caught up in the mauls and rucks that were previously the preserve of the forwards.

Your child's position

Almost the first question any parent asks their child when they start playing a new team sport is 'So, what position are you playing?' This demonstration of supposed knowledge usually leads to you falling flat on your face when your child replies, 'I don't know, I think I'm a back' or 'I think I'm a forward.'

Since the game is new to them, too, it may take several weeks before they play in a consistent position on the field and develop any understanding of that role within the team; until then, they will probably have no idea what position they are playing. Eventually, however, they will find their regular place.

For younger players, it is traditional that the larger children will become forwards and the smaller or faster ones will join the backs. Later on this may all change as players change shape through the teenage years, and your slim little back can quite easily turn into a hulking brute of a forward over the space of a couple of rugby seasons.

However, it will generally remain true that if they move fast over the ground, they will become a back, and if they tower over their peers or weigh a little more than average they could be more suited to the forwards group.

The smallest player on the pitch is frequently the scrum-half. Quite why the smallest player should be the one who has to get closest to the big heavy forwards we have never understood, but there it is.

Certain positions on the rugby pitch require particular physiques, and the following general descriptions may help you pick out a player at a glance as you start to watch your first season of rugby.

Forwards

The players known as the forwards make up the three rows of a scrum: front row forwards, second row forwards and back row forwards.

Front row forwards

These players include the hooker and the prop forwards (tight-head and loose-head). Tradition has it that forwards do not need the looks of a Hollywood film star to play well. To be an effective front row forward, a player should preferably have very long arms and no neck. Players with normal arms and necks tend to play elsewhere – regardless of their looks.

The tight-head prop is the player who has opposition heads either side of his in the scrum, and the loose-head is at the other edge with one side of his head open to the air.

Front row forwards are renowned for their volatile tempers – they are best left well alone as things can become awkward if they're roused.

Second row forwards (locks)

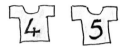

The second row forwards help lock the scrum together, but their main claim to fame on the field is the ability to use their extra height in *line-outs*.

A line-out is a set piece of play where the ball is thrown by the hooker from the sideline towards the two rows of forwards. Obviously a tall second row forward will be best placed to catch the ball. It is this height differential that also gives lock forwards their other reputation – that of being highly sociable.

Their ability to catch a barmaid's eye develops much earlier than their peers, as does their ability to hoodwink a barman into believing they are over the drinking age limit when in truth they still have a couple of years to go before reaching the officially sanctioned age for such pursuits.

They can thus be relied on to get in a round of drinks no matter who is paying – merely asking for a pint as a small fee for this service. No wonder they have a reputation for joining in the end-of-match celebrations at the bar earlier in their lives than the rest of their team-mates. Rugby players maintain a formidable reputation for their ability to consume vast quantities of beer, although this is changing with healthy diets being emphasised at senior levels of the game.

Back row forwards

Not to be confused with the backs, the back row forwards are made up of the number 8 and two flankers or wing forwards at numbers 6 and 7. The back row players are expected to use their brains as well as their brawn. The flankers are the enemies of the opposition half-backs, whose lives are under constant threat from their crunching tackles. There is a blindside flanker at number 6 and an openside flanker at number 7.

The position of the blindside flanker depends on the proximity of a *touch line*, so if the scrum takes place close to the left-hand touch line, the blindside flanker will be closest to that touch line. If they are attacking or defending on the right-hand side, the blindside flanker's position will relate to the player standing on the right-hand side of the scrum. The openside flanker always lines up on the side which has a wide open space ahead of him. In other words, they swap position names, depending on where the scrum is taking place, although the players themselves maintain their fixed positions on either side of the scrum throughout.

The number 8 keeps the scrum together and controls the release of the ball once it has been heeled back through the legs of the scrum by the hooker – or at least that is the theory.

The back row forwards tend to be popular positions in the early stages of learning the game. Young players discover they don't like having someone else's head crammed up against their backsides and prefer standing at the back of the scrum. Number 8 is frequently given the role of team captain as he can muster his troops well from this position.

Incidentally, flankers have a well-deserved reputation for being excellent blood donors. Sadly, little of this makes it as far as the national transfusion service, most being spilt over rugby shirts and fields. If play is stopped for an injury, it's a pretty good bet that the player on the floor will be a bleeding flanker – assuming the full-back is not involved.

Backs – their roles and play

Traditionally, each player has a set number designating their role in the team. However, numbers worn by teams vary considerably these days, with some clubs using letters of the alphabet and senior players having squad numbers that greatly exceed 15. The following diagram shows the traditional way that backs would line up at the *kick-off* or behind the scrum, with the standard numbering associated with their positions. You can see that this group of players stands behind the forwards, and they are expected to run towards their opposition or tackle them as required.

The backs consist of number 9, the scrum-half; number 10, the fly-half; number 11, on the left wing; number 12, the inside centre; number 13, the outside centre; and at number 14 there's the right wing. Numbers 11, 12, 13 and 14 are also sometimes known as the three-quarter backs or three-quarters. Completing the team, number 15 is the full-back.

Half-backs

These are the fly-half (or outside half) at number 10 and the scrum-half at number 9. You'll rapidly learn that both the scrum-half and the fly-half think they are in charge of the game and team tactics, which can make for interesting conflicts during the course of a game.

They care deeply about things like ball pressure (obviously a soft ball bounces less than a well pumped-up ball). They discuss crosswinds and options, things the majority of the team couldn't give a toss about.

Generally they are regarded as more intelligent than their team-mates, and they are frequently expected to make end-of-season reports on behalf of their team at junior level. Rugby supporters like you can help, though, and to assist you, we've included a useful score sheet at the back of this book if you want to help your young player complete this task.

Scrum-half

The main role of scrum-halves is to act as the link between the forwards and the backs. Of all the players on the pitch, the scrum-half probably does the most running about as he dashes from one situation to the next to link forwards and backs together. They are therefore particularly fit individuals in a rugby team.

As explained earlier, the scrum-half is frequently the smallest person on the pitch. He's the one you see throwing the ball at the feet of the group hug and then dashing to the back of this group to pick the ball out again (which seems such a waste of time until you fully understand what's going on). He will then throw it back to the fly-half who may even pass it on to the three-quarters to run the ball.

This is often done with what looks like an attempt on his part to defy gravity and fly, which then leads to him landing flat on the muddy ground whilst the forwards rampage over the top of him to get to the ball.

Actually, this is one of the funnier sights available to supporters watching a game – and generally the scrum-half survives unharmed despite the rampaging of the forwards. As a result of these plays, the scrum-halves are generally the children with the most understanding mothers, as their kit will usually be the muddiest (except perhaps for the full-back – more on this later).

A flying half-back

As part of their role, scrum-halves frequently kick the ball away from the opposition to gain territory. The ball can, for instance, be given a short, shallow kick forwards, bouncing it along the ground under the opponents' feet. This is known as a *grubber kick* and will force the opposition to stop and turn, and they will find it more difficult to collect or gather the ball from the ground. In many ways this is the reverse of the *up-and-under* kick described later on. Alternatively, the ball can be kicked up and over an opponent, and then the player can dash after it and pick it up again. This is known as *chip and chase*.

Another standard scrum-half kick is a *box kick* which goes backwards high over his shoulder while he is facing his own attacking team members. It's similar to the scissor kick used in football. The box kick is used in tight attacking or defensive situations and always surprises the opposition when the ball emerges from the scrum-half, flying back at speed over his shoulder, and they then have to turn and chase it back down the pitch.

Fly-half

Usually one of the quickest thinkers on the pitch, the fly-half is responsible for ultimately deciding whether it is worth running the ball – either individually or by passing it down the line of backs – or whether the team would get farther down the pitch if he kicked the ball towards the opposition and risked losing it to them after it lands.

As a result of these options, fly-halves are frequently blamed for the ball being lost to the other team and need great strength of character to withstand the complaints of their team-mates when they make a wrong decision. Of course, when the decision goes well and the ball bounces neatly into touch to set up a line-out near the try line, they are everyone's heroes.

Some fly-halves have self-belief beyond their skill set and can be seen dashing off with the ball, traversing the pitch at speed and confusing the opposition (and their team-mates, too, occasionally). Their natural inclination to run with the ball being hardwired, they sometimes do that over and over again until a series of crunching tackles reminds them that they do have other options, including passing the ball to their team-mates.

They are also fearsome tacklers, despite their sometimes small stature in comparison to the sturdy forwards they glibly choose to tackle. Sadly, this can result in injuries, and wounded fly-halves abound at senior level. Jonny Wilkinson of England was a prime example when, despite his brilliance, he was frequently injured and unable to play. Happily, at more junior levels injuries are rarer.

Three-quarter backs (or just the three-quarters)

These are the inside and outside centres and the two players on the wing – four players in all.

Centres or centre three-quarter backs

The centres (numbers 12 and 13) line up outside the fly-half and are next in line to receive the ball as it's being passed down the line of backs who are attacking the try line.

If the ball is being run well down the pitch and there are not many members of the opposition team ahead of them, they will occasionally even pass it out to the wings, those speedy individuals (not always particularly large members of the junior-level team) who can be relied on to sprint for the line and score tries if they are not tackled first. Centres are also aggressive tacklers, and all opposition backs (and even some forwards) dread a tackle from these players.

They also have to use their intelligence to decide which way to pass the ball to avoid their team being tackled by the opposition, which would of course result in them losing the ball.

One of centres frequently looks upon himself as a *crash ball* specialist and will set up attacks by running straight at the opposition tacklers without any sign of fear for his own personal safety. The centres are also capable of giving their team-mates passes that will clearly result in them getting tackled and indeed may result in their possible injury due to the number of opposition they face, rather than facing up to the tackle themselves. These are commonly known as *hospital passes*. You can understand why.

Like their fly-half team-mates, they sometimes take a decision to dash off in the opposite direction across the pitch on receiving the ball. You'll rapidly discover that this bold manoeuvre, at least at junior level, invariably results in the centre running straight into the *pack* of opposition forwards, getting tackled and losing the ball, much to his team-mates' disgust.

Wingers (wings or wing three-quarters)

The wings (numbers 11 and 14) can get through an entire game of rugby without ever touching the ball thanks to a combination of the forwards not letting the backs see the ball in the first place and the centres not wanting to pass the ball out to them but rather preferring to disappear off in the opposite direction across the pitch as described already.

Just occasionally, though, little wings will get the chance to sprint all the way down the length of the pitch, skirting the danger of the touch line, side stepping and dodging their way around lumbering forwards and exhausted backs in the opposition, leaving them trailing in their wake until they eventually cross the try line and score that elusive prize – a try.

Cheers from the crowd are never more heartfelt than when one of these valuable little members of the team scores in this fashion.

While junior wings are traditionally small and speedy, the arrival of Jonah Lomu of New Zealand on the international scene towards the end of the 20th century changed that trend forever. Senior-level players are now quite tall but still remain speedy individuals. Top-flight Olympic sprinters are taller these days, too – just a sign of the times, perhaps.

Wingers definitely think of themselves as the sprinters of the rugby squad and spend hours running up and down the pitch, hardly ever touching the ball. By the time they reach senior level, their patience has generally run out, and wings may track across the pitch sometimes switching positions with the other wing to ensure they get to receive the passed ball at least once in a match. However, at junior level such independence is frowned upon, as part of their role is defensive, and moving from their allotted side of the pitch could result in the opposition scoring a try without being challenged.

Given how cold they can get just standing around waiting for the rugby ball to reach them, it's a miracle they can actually catch it and run from a standing start to score tries. If your offspring is a wing, you'll always get to see plenty of them, as you can usually stand on the touch line next to them throughout the match, but please don't distract them by chatting to them or offering sustenance or warm drinks during a game, however tempting that might be. They will always thaw out later.

Full-back

Finally we come to the full-back, the number 15 in the team, who seemingly enjoys getting stamped all over by the opposition when cleanly catching high balls. He will bounce up from the heap of players, waving away any trainer who might want to treat any wounds sustained in the process, and then, having cleared the ball by kicking it back down the pitch, he will search the skies again for the next high ball to catch.

Full-backs really hope their clearance kicks will give them a chance to run back at the opposition, despite the high risk of being trampled underfoot yet again as the attacking team chases after the ball, too, but this option rarely works out in their favour.

If your offspring frequently returns from rugby practices or matches claiming that the rest of the team have blamed them for losing the match, it is a pretty certain bet that he is a full-back. As the last line of defence for the team, if all the others have failed to stop a marauding attack from the opposition, they can be relied upon to throw themselves selflessly at the feet of a thundering attacker in a desperate attempt to halt the opposition's progress towards the try line.

All too frequently they will fail, as their opposite number is likely to be

(a) heavier, (b) taller and (c) coming towards them at great speed.

On a good day, however, they can kick the ball long and hard to get their team out of trouble and halt attacking moves from the opposition. Sometimes they even set up good running tries with the careful placement of a kick that a winger can chase down, catch and then run with the ball to score at the opposite end of the pitch. Because of their long-kicking ability, the full-back can also take the *conversion kicks* and *penalty kicks* – although this role is frequently shared with the fly-half.

However, there is another, less obvious reason for a young player choosing to become a full-back. During those first lessons at school or first practices at a rugby club, they may conclude that this position right at the back of the team (somewhat similar to a goalkeeper in association football) affords the best position from which to avoid any action whatsoever and keep them from getting hurt. They will eventually learn that this is definitely not the case, but for a brief period of time, they will enjoy playing rugby without any contact – indeed, they may hardly touch the ball or the opposition at all.

So now that they have a position, what happens next?

Initially younger players will learn to pass the ball from hand to hand and will play *touch* or *tag rugby*, also known as *mini rugby* at rugby clubs and schools where young players can start to learn the game.

The England Rugby organisation now gets kids involved through the Kids First Rugby initiative. This aims to break the sport down into bite-sized chunks in order to ease understanding and enhance the skills of even the youngest players.

It is aimed at under 7s, under 8s and under 9s, and the scheme has been trialled over the past three years and incorporates new rules, such as smaller-sided games, that encourage young players to keep the ball in hand, developing their passing and running in the process.

You can learn all about this new initiative at

>> www.englandrugby.com/news/video-ruckley-launches-kids-first-rugby-twickenham-1264883/
   or
>> www.internationalminirugby.com
   or
>> www.englandrugby.com/mm/Document/MyRugby/Education/01/30/51/33/tagtotacklelessons1-10_English.pdf

For worried parents, touch rugby merely means that small children will not be learning how to tackle (or bring down) their opponents just yet, but rather will just touch them lightly with a hand in order to trigger the passing of the ball to another player. Failing that, they have to hand the ball over to the opposition on instruction from the referee. Tag rugby involves a tag attached to a belt – a system we explain in the glossary.

However, touch rugby does not last forever, and before long they will be tackling their friends and crashing happily to the ground with them – in most homes this is known as the start of 'the washing season'.

Washing season and kit purchase

Washing and cleaning tips

So, your kid has taken up playing rugby, and guess what? They get muddy!

Once your young player has mastered tackling, your washing load will instantly increase as muddy rugby shorts, socks and shirts are brought home after every games lesson (and practice) and are needed, clean and pressed, frequently for the next day. The advantages of having a second string (or perhaps second-hand) set of kit clothing to save the panic washing and drying of kit will rapidly become apparent. Of course, if your children are away at boarding school, then it is poor Matron and her team who will have to tackle the laundry – lucky you.

Rugby kit is specially designed to take rough treatment and responds well to all the standard biological and stain-removing washing products available on the market. The joy of a combination of a good stain remover and a biological washing powder or liquid will usually guarantee clean kit for your keen rugby player, without too much effort on your part.

More old-fashioned ways of keeping kit clean still work, of course, and these may be useful if your player has any skin problems that preclude biological products from being used or your waste water system doesn't allow you to use them.

These include soaking blood-stained items in strongly salted water overnight before washing. When most of the stain has gone, you can rub the residue with a paste of table salt mixed with a small amount of water. Soak the item in washing detergent for a few more hours, then wash as usual. You probably already know that you should never use hot water on blood stains (or wine stains for that matter) until the stain has faded or been diluted, or it will be sealed in permanently.

The traditional techniques for removing other stains include:

Grass: Sponge with warm soapy water and a little methylated spirit or eucalyptus oil.

Mud: Just soak first in cold water until dissolved, then wash well.

Perspiration: Dissolve two aspirin tablets in water to remove stains, or mix a tablespoon (15 ml) of white vinegar in a third of a pint (200 ml) of water and sponge the affected area, then soak in detergent, and then wash as normal.

If these more labour-intensive methods don't appeal, you can always use a biological cleaner first as a prewash and then wash again in non-biological products.

Of course some boys seem able to play in mud-caked and hardened kit from day to day without ever bringing it home, but the school teachers and club coaches soon put a stop to this and will suggest that getting their kit added to the family washing load is greatly preferable to gassing the rest of the team.

If you are lucky (and the teachers and coaches continue to hold sway), your small child will have a shower after each rugby training session and then at least they will return home fairly clean. If you are not so lucky, they will change rapidly into their school uniform or casual clothing before anyone notices they haven't showered, and you may catch them scratching the mud off their legs whilst trying to do homework, watching television or playing computer games later in the day.

At this stage, I suggest you insist that they show you their mud-covered limbs and then force them into the bathroom as quickly as possible. The earlier you can catch them, the less fine mud dust will be found on the carpet the next morning!

I imagine this is not generally a problem girls will present to their parents, but forewarned is forearmed.

Kit purchase

Kit is supplied from various sources, including online suppliers. See our list in the web links section at the back of this book. At school, the school's own sports shop may supply kit at reasonable prices, or the local school uniform shop may be another source. As previously mentioned, you should bear in mind that you will need at least two sets of kit, as sports teachers have a habit of planning practice sessions just before matches against other schools when your child will then be expected to turn up in pristine kit to meet their opposition.

At public schools, pupils will also need house colour rugby shirts as well as school shirts, but it's well worth checking if your school or club has a second-hand shop. It's not a cheap thing this kit lark, and that's without even starting on rugby boots.

Boots

Rugby boots have changed considerably in the past few decades and are generally interchangeable with football boots these days. However, players must change their studs to the safety version specifically designed for use in rugby. These studs are designed to grip the surface of the pitch without injuring other players when they come in close proximity during play. If traditional football boot studs are retained, they could cause untold damage to fellow players in a ruck or maul situation.

Studs come in two lengths to allow for both muddy and dry grassy conditions and need to be changed before a match, depending on the state of the pitch. In the end, most players play in the shorter studs most of the time as they find it difficult to run in the longer studs. Some football boots come fitted with blades instead of studs, but these are not at all appropriate for rugby, because they don't give enough traction on a muddy pitch.

Headgear

Headgear has also changed greatly in recent years, and many young players are now encouraged to wear the scrum caps that were previously only worn by one or two members of the scrum front and second rows. Anxious mothers will be pleased to learn that this protective headgear has become acceptable for all, and players who wear scrum caps are considered wise rather than wimpish if they sport them nowadays.

Body armour

Although padded undershirts are often used at senior level to protect shoulders from damage in the tackle and scrum, they are very much discouraged for junior players. It is really not sensible to encourage your young player to use such items until they are secure in tackling without them; they are far less likely to tackle too hard without added protection than with it.

Senior players seem to be getting injured these days because they think their padded shoulders and scrum caps will protect them, and it's very important that junior players don't adopt these protective devices too soon. Tackling safely is always possible when players know their limitations, and any protection that lessens a sense of self-preservation should be avoided. It's absolutely vital to emphasise the importance of learning to tackle without protection first to ensure that safe tackling skills are learned from an early age.

Protection for the teeth

Mouthguards, or gum shields, are essential. Schools and clubs advise proper fitting by a dentist, with adjustments before each season, to avoid unnecessary mouth injuries and discomfort from ill-fitting 'ready-made' products. Your young player will be pleased to know that dentists are well aware of the need for style in a mouthguard, and for a reasonable sum your young player can wear a smile to frighten the boldest forward in the opposition.

Personally, we were always particularly fond of the single white tooth in the middle of a black mouthguard – it's always amusing for the spectators.

The final article of clothing, a total mystery to most women but an essential piece of sports kit for the men in their lives, is the athletic support, or jock strap. This flimsy contraption is designed to maintain equilibrium for the more sensitive parts of the male anatomy and is worn under the shorts.

The first visit to a sports supplier to purchase this particular piece of kit is something that may well be better left to a father, uncle or grandfather, but all too frequently this task will fall to a mother. Thankfully, these days the advent of slip underwear and fitted boxer shorts means the need to wear an athletic support is less essential for the very young players, but it's worth bearing in mind that this might be something you get asked for, and I hope that knowledge of its existence may (if nothing else) minimise the embarrassment for both parties.

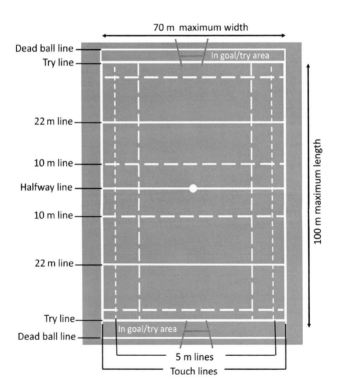

The game

We hope you are beginning to have a feel for what Rugby Union is all about, so it is time to have a go at describing an actual match. Just to make things as simple as possible for you, let's start by describing the ground on which it is played – the pitch.

The pitch

Rugby is played on a field up to 100-metres (330 ft) long and 70-metres (230 ft) wide with H-shaped goal posts on each goal line. You can see what a rugby pitch looks like from a bird's-eye view in the diagram.

The pitch is divided into several sections. At each end there is a section behind the goal posts marked by a white line. Between the edge of the pitch, on the goal line and level with the posts, and through to this white line is where a try can be scored; this is known as the *in goal*, or *try area*. The goal line can also be called the try line, and the line behind the posts is called the *dead ball line*. If the ball keeps on travelling until it passes the dead ball line, it is no longer in play.

No one can score by touching the ball down once it has passed that line, and it will be returned to the 22-metre line for a *drop-out* kick by the defending team. However, if a defender kicks or takes the ball over the dead ball line, this will result in a 5-metre scrum being awarded with his opposition putting in the ball.

In addition to the try area, the pitch is also marked with a centre or halfway line and a spot through which the starting kick-off is taken. Other lines marked on the pitch include 22-metre lines and 10-metre lines, and along the length of the pitch there are lines marked at 5 and 15 metres into the pitch. The touch lines are the lines down the sides of the pitch; line-outs take place here when the ball has been kicked or knocked into touch. But more importantly this is where you will be standing as a spectator.

Supporters stand on or next to the touch lines during a game to cheer on their team. Depending on your child's or partner's position, you may choose to stand at a particular point on the touch line in order to see as much as possible of them as they play in a match.

Of course, if the player you've come to watch is the scrum-half, you're going to get a lot of exercise – you'll be dashing from one end of the pitch to the other to keep track of the action. Not only is the scrum-half the fittest player on the pitch, his keen supporters will need to be pretty fit as well.

Playing a game

Games are played in two halves of 40 minutes, with a short break at half-time when teams swap ends for the second half of the match, sometimes taking time for refreshments and changing into clean shirts and shorts, depending on the weather.

Referees keep strict time records, stopping their watches when play halts for whatever reason to ensure exactly 40 minutes of actual play takes place in each half.

As we explained earlier, when playing rugby, the first and most important rule or Law to learn is that the ball may only be passed laterally or backwards, never forwards towards the opposing team's goal line.

In fact, the ball can only be moved forwards in three ways: (1) by kicking it, (2) by a player running while holding onto it or (3) within a scrum, ruck or maul.

Only the player with the ball may be tackled or rucked, and defenders cannot tackle or even block any other players. Blocking or tripping is a foul called obstruction that will get penalised by the referee.

When a ball is knocked forwards to the ground by players using their arms or hands, a knock-on infringement occurs, and play is restarted with a scrum. All players are allowed to kick the ball forwards in an attempt to gain territory, and we give full details of this type of play later in this book.

Every game starts with a kick-off, where a drop kick is used from the centre of the halfway line to start the match. The ball must travel at least 10 metres away from the kick-off point towards the opposition goal line before it hits the ground for this kick to be within the Laws, and if this doesn't happen, it is penalised with a scrum. It's obviously helpful that the 10-metre lines are marked on the pitch. If the ball goes the correct distance and is picked up by either the attacking or defending team, it can then be passed between them, and this is known as *open play*.

Once a young player has mastered the basic rules of passing and tackling (more on which later), the more complicated rules and regulations will start to enter into their skills.

Touching down – scoring a touchdown or try

In order to touch the ball down and score a try, the player carrying the ball merely has to push it down on the grass inside the in-goal area over the try line. They can also do this by diving towards the ground with the ball safely in their hands.

In recent years, a young England rugby winger called Chris Ashton has developed something of a reputation for scoring in this way (not unlike our flying half-back on page 27). Alternatively, if the ball has been kicked over the goal line, players can race and dive after it to slap the ball down onto the ground with either one or both hands.

The vision of a speeding half-back racing over the line and launching himself at the ball is another of the amusing sights available to watching parents, perhaps only bettered by the sight of a scrum-half trying to peer over the shoulders or through the legs of a particularly large second-row or back-row forward to see where the ball has gone in a scrum or at a line-out.

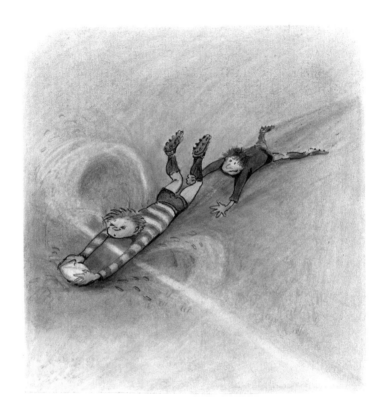

The most important aspect of try scoring is that the scorer must use downward pressure on the ball as it hits the ground over the try line, or the try won't count. Television replays of tries frequently spend many minutes trying to establish if downward pressure has been put on the ball before a try is allowed. At amateur level of course, just the referee and his assistants have to make these decisions, without the benefit of video replays, and can only award tries when they clearly see the ball being grounded with proper downward pressure from the scorer.

Tackling skills

The standard tackle involves one player grasping another around or below the waist to pull him to the ground. As we've already said, players are only allowed to tackle an opposing player who is holding onto the ball (known as the *ball carrier*). They do this by holding onto them and bringing them down to the ground, until either one or two knees are on the ground or they are sitting on the ground or even landing on top of another player who is on the ground.

Tacklers cannot tackle above their opponent's shoulder line (the neck and head are considered out of bounds), and tacklers have to attempt to wrap their arms around the player being tackled to complete the tackle. Tackles made above the shoulder are termed *high tackles*, and these are penalised by the referee giving a penalty kick to the opposition.

It is illegal to push, shoulder-charge, or to trip a player using feet or legs, but hands may be used (this is referred to as a *tap-tackle* or *ankle-tap*). Shirts are sometimes torn at junior levels as shirt-grabbing is easier to

manage when young players are first learning how to tackle. Players will soon discover that while grabbing at a shirt may help to topple a slight running back, it will rarely have any effect on the more robust and sturdy forwards.

Swinging players around by the arm can also be effective when size and weight differences are greater in young players moving into their early teenage years, but this is obviously discouraged as dangerous for all involved. Some young players grow and mature much earlier than others, and this makes size differences quite noticeable and low tackles more complicated for the taller members of the team. In an ideal world all tackles should take place around or below the waist.

Tap tackle

This is a perfectly legal means of tackling a running ball carrier, by tapping the back of their feet or legs whilst they are running to upset their balance and trip them up. In truth, the runner is much less likely to get hurt than the tackler, who risks being kicked in the face as he reaches for the speeding player's heels. Experienced full-backs are masters of this masochistic form of tackling and proudly sport the resultant black eyes.

Kicking the ball

Whilst the ball is traditionally carried in rugby, it is also kicked in several situations, especially by the scrum-half and fly-half.

(1) Conversion kicks

When a try has been scored, the team's best kicker (usually the fly-half or full-back) will try to convert that try by kicking the ball over the crossbar and between the posts. The ball is always placed back on the pitch exactly in line with the point where the try was scored, but the kicker can move as far backwards (away from the goal) as they want, before taking the kick. If the try is scored near the touch line, for instance, the kicker usually goes back a good distance to widen the angle of the kick in order to score. If the try is scored underneath the posts, kickers will only need to go back a few metres to allow themselves an easy kick to score the conversion.

(2) Penalty kicks

These are taken whenever the opposition has broken the Laws in some way (see the infringements section). The kick is taken through the point where the infringement occurred and can either be taken by the ball being placed on the ground, sometimes on top of a small mound of sand or earth or more usually using a plastic kicking tee, and then kicked. Alternatively, the kicker can hold the ball in his hands and drop it to kick it in the air after it has hit the ground (a drop kick). Penalty kicks which cross the touch lines will be followed by a line-out with the same team that took the penalty kick taking the throw-in.

Penalty kicks taken in front of the goal posts can result in points being scored if the ball succeeds in passing through the posts in the required fashion. Some senior players have the ability to kick penalty goals from behind the halfway line, but they are a rare breed. In Europe, Jonny

Wilkinson of England and Chris Patterson of Scotland both became famous for their unerring ability with conversions, drop goals and penalty kicks. In Wilkinson's case, this included his dramatic last-minute drop goal which won the Rugby World Cup for England in 2003. You can find it online by searching for "Jonny Wilkinson Rugby World Cup winning drop kick".

(3) Clearance kicks

These can be taken at any time during the game and are normally used to improve a side's position on the pitch. These include the grubber kick and box kick that we described earlier as being used by the scrum-half as a regular part of his play. As long as the ball bounces in the field of play before going into touch, a throw-in is taken by a member of the opposition team at the point where the ball crosses the touch line as designated by the touch judge, or anywhere on the touch line farther down the field away from the kicker.

Usually such kicks will result in a line-out being taken; however, players from the team entitled to throw the ball in, who are quick off the mark, can throw the ball back onto the pitch to their team-mates before the opposition arrives to force a line-out (as long as the ball passes the 5-metre line before another player touches it). This is known as a quick throw-in, but the ball must travel back towards their own goal line if a player takes a quick throw-in.

In addition, if a player is standing inside his own 22-metre area and kicks directly into touch (i.e. without the ball bouncing in-field first), a line-out will be taken by the opposition where the ball went into touch. However, if the ball is kicked into touch directly by a player standing outside his team's 22-metre area, or if his team-mates have carried or passed the ball back into the 22-metre area just prior to the kick being taken, then the line-out is taken level to where the original kick was made, and no advantage is gained by the kicker's team.

So the kicker has to be aware of his own position on the pitch and judge the distance very carefully before taking one of these kicks to ensure his team gains an advantage.

(4) Very high (clearance) kicks

These are used to help the attacking team move towards the try line in the hope that team-mates will sprint after the high ball and catch it or at least compete for it. In some parts of the world these kicks are known as bombs, which gives you a feeling for how high they go and how quickly they come back down towards the waiting players. These kicks are also nicknamed 'up-and-unders' in Rugby League football and 'Garryowens' in Union. Some people think they were named after Ireland's Garryowen Rugby Union club in Limerick that had popularised the technique. Others say the kick was named after Garfield Owen, a famous Welsh full-back from the 1950s who was renowned for using the technique. Whichever way it came about, it's a common term that's good to understand if you hear it in a TV or radio commentary.

It might seem that the backs are giving the ball to the opposition by doing this, but pity the defending player trying to catch the swirling ball as it plummets towards him from high in the sky whilst a horde of speeding backs and enormous forwards charge towards him. He really should stand little chance of catching it cleanly, and the attacking team frequently goes on to pick up the ball and run with it again. Of course, it is traditional for full-backs to be the defending catchers – no wonder they live in fear of their team-mates blaming them for losing the game.

Forward play

For the forwards (or the pack, as they are sometimes called), forward play will include line-outs, mauls and rucks as well as scrums. The main role of the forwards is to wrest the ball from the opposition through these various modes of play. If a ball goes off the side of the pitch (i.e. over the touch line), a line-out will be taken.

Line-outs

Many disagreements will occur at the start of a line-out since it is never the team that kicked, threw or dropped the ball over the touch line that gets to throw it back in; it is always their opposition (exactly as in association football). A ball can, of course, be accidentally touched by opposition players after a kick is taken and before it crosses the touch line, and this often results in disagreements as to whose throw-in it is going to be, especially at junior matches.

However, once it has been established which team is taking the throw-in, which in a match will be clearly shown by the referee's colleagues (the touch judges), it is the job of that team's hooker to throw the ball straight, over the heads of and between the two rows of forwards.

The forwards from both teams must stand in what look like queue lines, forming two straight lines standing about one metre apart. This gap must be maintained until the ball is thrown in, and teams can be penalised for not maintaining the gap. The opposition hooker normally stands close to the throwing hooker until the ball has been thrown.

A regular line-out will involve all the eight forwards – seven in each of the two lines and the hookers separate, of course. A shortened line-out can reduce that number to as few as two in each line, but this rarely happens, although line-outs do frequently reduce to four from each team.

Sometimes a shortened line-out is used to allow the hooker to throw the ball right over the row of forwards to link up with another fast-moving forward or a speeding back who will catch the ball and charge off with it towards the try line.

The attacking team uses secret codes to confirm which player will be catching the ball and strange shouts of 'Himalayas' and 'Alps' or codes like '137' can be heard being yelled over the line of forwards before the hooker throws the ball. This gives the attacking team an advantage at the start of the match, but oppositions frequently work out what the codes mean and are able to contest effectively for the ball as the game progresses.

Once the ball has been thrown by the hooker, players from both sets of forwards will help one of their pack to leap high in the air to catch the ball as it passes over and between their heads. Generally a second row lock forward (if you remember, they are likely to be the tallest members of the team) is helped up into the air by two of his team-mates and ideally catches the ball, landing back on the ground clutching it to his chest. If he catches the ball safely, he then turns his back on the opposition to set up a maul or a ruck (we'll explain the difference between these later) until the ball emerges from the back of the forwards group to be passed back to the scrum-half.

It's important to know that no player who jumps for the ball in a line-out is allowed to be tackled until they are safely down on the ground again. Line-outs are frequently turned into penalty kicks when the jumping player is pulled, held, shoved or leant on by his opposite number before his feet have touched the ground again.

If the leaping forwards are unable to take the ball cleanly from the hooker's throw, they can tap the ball down towards a receiver, a player who stands next to the line-out to wait for such a pass, usually the scrum-half. However, if they do this, they are only allowed to use either their inside arm and hand or both arms and hands, never their outside arm alone.

Once the receiver has the ball, he will hopefully pass it out to the fly-half who will then pass it on to the other backs for them to run the ball towards the try line. Alternatively, he may kick the ball as far as possible down the pitch to gain territory (a clearance kick). This is generally an unpopular move with supporters, as it frequently results in possession of the ball transferring immediately to the opposition, thus halting an attack.

The line-out is the part of the game where infringements regularly occur (including pushing, closing the gap, pulling down the opposition). If, after an attempted line-out, the ball is immediately handed to the opposition to kick, you can be pretty certain that the team you're supporting has committed one of these infringements.

Another minor infringement in the line-out, which would result in a scrum being taken, could be a knock-on (where, you may remember, a player drops or knocks the ball forwards onto the ground with hands or arms). You will notice that knock-ons also occur when backs are running with the ball and pass it to another player who does not quite catch the ball but drops it forwards.

If the hooker is asked to throw the ball again at a line-out, it may be that they did not manage to throw the ball in straight between and over the lines of forwards. When your young player is still learning the game, school and club referees will frequently let them have a second go. Once the rules have been learned, however, this would be penalised, and the opposition would be offered the choice of a scrum or another line-out, and this time their hooker will get to throw or put the ball in.

The final way a hooker can throw the ball in is to virtually pass it straight to the nearest forward in the line – this is most frequently done at shortened line-outs. If the line-out is taking place close to the try line, this can result in the forward catching the ball and launching himself over the line to score a try, frequently to the amazement of the opposition players who are expecting a high throw over their heads. However, the ball must always travel at least 5 metres from the hooker before it is touched by another player.

Quick throw-ins, as we described earlier, are sometimes taken in an attempt to keep the ball moving, but if they fail to travel far enough (i.e. over the 5-metre line), they will result in the ball being lost to the opposition for them to throw in at a standard line-out, so players need to be pretty sure they will get the throw-in right if they plan to take a quick one. The ball must always travel back towards the player's own goal line (as if it were a standard pass), and the player must be certain his team is entitled to take the throw-in before attempting this manoeuvre.

Scrums

No, they're not just a team bonding exercise or group hug. Scrums are used as a way of restarting the game when the ball has gone out of play, either when the ball becomes unplayable in a ruck or maul (explained later) or following a minor infringement of the Laws.

The scrum (or scrummage) consists of the three rows of forward players from each team, and the front row (tight-head prop, hooker and loose-head prop) will *bind* with the front row of the opposition so that their heads interlock, forming a kind of *tunnel* under their heads and between their feet. This is where you will realise the tight-head and loose-head prop names have a reason; the tight-head prop ends up with his head enclosed on both sides by opposition heads, while the loose-head prop only has one side of his head against the opposition.

A scrum always occurs after a stoppage in play, usually because a foul has taken place (this can be anything from a knock-on or crooked throw-in to accidental offside). It can be an alternative option to a free kick or line-out.

Scrums can never take place within 5 metres of either the goal line or the touch lines, so don't be surprised if the referee walks away from either of these zones to place a scrum farther away from the location of an infringement.

All the backs, except the scrum-half, retreat away from the position of the scrum and, from the new supporter's view, they seem to pretty much leave the forwards to get on with it. The ball is then thrown into the middle of the gap (or tunnel) between the two teams by the scrum-half, and both sides must compete to try and *hook* the ball and send it backwards through the scrum with their feet. During the scrum, both sets of forwards will push against their opposition in an attempt to gain possession of the ball. You will hear television and radio commentators referring to this as 'contesting the scrum'.

The scrum-half throws the ball into the tunnel, and once the ball hits the ground, the forwards are allowed to raise their feet to try to hook it back. Lifting feet before the ball is on the ground will result in more penalties being imposed.

Once possession of the ball has been secured, a team can keep the ball on the ground and inside the scrum and attempt to drive the opposition backwards down the field with sheer brute force. When the ball tracks back through the scrum and reaches the hindmost foot in the scrum (normally the number 8's foot), the ball can be picked up and carried forward or passed.

This is where the scrum-half is a key player – being responsible for putting the ball in and for picking it out of the back of the scrum. You should be aware that once the ball is picked up, the forwards are allowed to let go of each other and tackle the ball carrier. You will frequently hear a shout of 'out' when the scrum-half lets his team know they can unbind because the ball is back in open play.

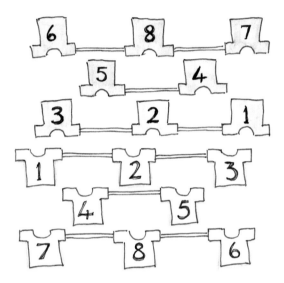

The forwards line up as shown in this diagram. As we've already explained, most rugby shirts are numbered to tally with specific positions on the field and in the scrum – like in the diagram. The loose-head prop (1) will always stand on the left-hand side of his team; the tight-head prop (3) is on the right. However, with senior teams playing squad numbers in rotation these days, sadly you can no longer guarantee that the man wearing number 9 is the scrum-half, or the number 8 shirt wearer is necessarily the back row man. However, at true amateur level, including school and mini rugby, the numbers still remain constant, and you should be able to work out where a player should be on the pitch by looking at their shirt number.

If this really interests you, there is more information on scrummaging skills at the following websites:

>> www.worldrugby.org

>> www.talkrugbyunion.co.uk/

>> www.rugby-sidestep-central.com/rugby-positions.html

A word of warning: If your tall player asks you for a bandage and sticky tape to tape their ears down before playing rugby, please don't be surprised. The discomfort they could incur as fellow forwards hug them, crushing their hips against their heads, or alternatively as they crush their own heads against the opposition's heads as the scrum comes together, will rapidly convince you that taping down their ears is the least of their problems. It should be noted, however, that most youthful forwards are not generally masochistic enough to do this, and only the toughest amongst these young players will take to taping their ears from an early age, especially as there now excellent scrum caps – World Rugby-approved headgear – that players have taken to wearing if they are in those difficult positions in the scrum.

>> See www.irbplayerwelfare.com/?documentid=52.

As a point of curiosity, the scrummage was adopted under its old name of scrimmage by the Americans to form a permanent part of their version of football. The word fell out of favour for Rugby Union but remains in regular use in the USA.

What really happens in a scrum – the referee's input

We've already given you a basic idea, but here's the detail of what goes on in the 'group hug' from the officials' standpoint. The scrum-half who is about to place or throw the ball into the scrum stands to the left of his own hooker, with the opposition scrum-half standing next to him but on the side of the scrum that his team are standing – he will be deemed offside if he stands behind the ball, even if it's inside the scrum.

The full explanation can be found here, but we'll try to simplify it for you:

>> laws.worldrugby.org/index.php?law=20

When a scrum is awarded, the referee will make a mark on the pitch with his boot, and the hookers must line up over this mark. An imaginary line runs through the mark parallel to the side lines for both hookers to stand on. Once the scrum has formed on both sides, the forwards all line up and wait for the instructions from the referee to 'crouch'. The individual packs then bind together, linking arms, and crouch down, standing approximately one arm's length apart. As the referee says 'bind', the two packs will come together binding heads in the front row. They mustn't push at this stage, however.

In addition to the front row heads binding, the two props will bind on either side of the scrum. The two tight-head props must bind on the opposing loose-head props by placing their right arms outside the left upper arms of the opponents. The tight-head props must grip the loose-head props' jerseys with right hands only on the back or side. The tight-head props must not grip the chest, arm, sleeve or collar of the opposing loose-head props and must not exert any downward pressure. You can see that there are very strict rules about binding, and improper binding is penalised with a penalty kick.

Then the referee says 'set', and at this command both packs steady themselves and prepare to push. Once the packs are steady, the referee will indicate to the scrum-half that he can put the ball into the tunnel – sometimes saying 'yes nine' (9 being the traditional number for a scrum-half). The scrum-half then puts the ball into the scrum straight down the channel between them, and the packs can push against each other. Hopefully the whole exercise will only take seconds, and the scrum will be both fast and safe for all involved as a result.

It is commonplace for the team that puts the ball into the scrum to retain possession of it, as the scrum-half and hooker can synchronise their actions so the latter knows when to strike to hook the ball back into his team's side of the scrum. At junior level the scrum-half will often tap the top of his hooker's head with the ball just before putting the ball into the tunnel so the hooker is ready to get the ball back. Of course right-footed hookers will find it easier to hook with their right foot as the ball comes into the tunnel, which also favours the throwing scrum-half's team.

With the ball in the scrum, the two hookers compete for possession, and with the entire pack jostling and pushing against each other it makes the task of hooking even more difficult. The hookers and props are all trying to hook the ball backwards with a foot or leg towards their own team, and the packs push against each other, sometimes twisting the scrum around in their efforts to gain control of the ball.

Gradually one side will get the ball to the back of the scrum, where the little scrum-half will have dashed – standing just behind the rearmost foot of the back row forwards in the scrum. Frequently he is tracked by his opposite number who hopes to steal the ball from him if possible, but the latter has to stay onside so number 8's control of the ball will be vital.

Usually, the scrum-half will dice with death at the back of the pack and pick the ball up from under his number 8's feet – not an easy act for a little person surrounded by enormous forwards, as we've previously said. Then he will pass it to the other backs, usually via the fly-half. Sometimes the number 8 will choose to pick the ball up himself and run off to set up a maul or ruck farther down the field.

This is not guaranteed to happen, however. If a scrum twists too far around (known as *wheeling the scrum*), the referee will blow his whistle and make the packs reset and start the process all over again. If the scrum twists round far enough, one team will end up offside, and the other team will be awarded a penalty kick. However, if the referee considers one team is causing the wheeling round deliberately, he will penalise them.

If the front row forwards all fall over on top of each other, bringing their pack with them, this is called a *collapsed scrum*, and if it is obviously accidental, the same scrum-half will get the chance to put in a second time, once all the forwards have stood up and reorganised themselves into a new scrum.

If, however, the referee considers that one team deliberately brought down the scrum, then he will give the ball to the opposition team to take a penalty kick. The ball can also be given to the opposition if the ball does not go straight into the tunnel (a Law that seems to be ignored quite a lot at more senior levels if the scrum-halves think the referee can't see their actions very clearly). Screams of 'not straight' can be heard echoing round the crowd who are seated on the side of the pitch that can see the entry transit of the ball into the tunnel, but unless the referee or his assistants see the offending move personally, they are unable to penalise it.

The opposition will also be given the ball if the referee believes the scrum-half is holding onto the ball for too long before putting it into the scrum. Yes, being a scrum-half is a job full of responsibility – you can be justly proud of your offspring or partner if they play in this key position on the pitch.

Mauls and rucks

More supporters new to the game of rugby ask, 'What's the difference between a maul and a ruck?' than almost any other question about rugby, especially when their young players are first learning the game.

So here goes with our simplified explanation: a *maul* occurs after a player holding the ball has come into contact with a tackler but remains on his feet. Once at least three players join or bind with the two original players, with the ball OFF the ground, a maul is formed, and players in possession will try to pass it between each other as they move forwards towards the opposition try line.

Sometimes they will choose to pass it back out to the backs to let them run with the ball, and the maul breaks up. More often than not, a rolling maul follows when the forwards move out and round as the ball is passed back through the maul. They peel off at the front and side and rejoin the maul at the back, gaining territory and gradually moving forwards down the pitch towards the try line with the ball in hand. Generally the ball is kept near the rear of the maul, so if progress gets halted by the opposition forwards, the ball can be easily passed out to the scrum-half for onward transmission to the backs.

The most common starting point for a maul is after a line-out, when the catching player will turn his back on the opposition, while his pack form around him and the ball is quickly passed back to the rearmost player of the maul. The pack will then attempt to push against the opposition pack and move the ball down the field inside the maul.

That's a ruck ... oh no it's a maul ... well maybe it's a ruck

A *ruck* occurs when the same group hug seems to be taking place, but now the ball is down ON the ground. Once three players have joined the huddle after a tackle has taken place, a ruck will be formed with the ball at their feet (and sometimes the original ball carrier and his tackler are on the ground, too – that can't be a pleasant place to be).

The two teams of forwards push against each other (much as they do in a scrum) to push their own team over the ball, using their boots to move the ball until it reappears at the rear of the rucking players, whereupon either the scrum-half (lucky little person) can pick it up and pass it out to the backs, or the final forward (frequently the number 8) can pick the ball up and start to run forwards with it again. As feet are being used to get the ball back, boots frequently come into contact with the players on the ground – hence the need for safety studs in rugby boots.

You should note that the ball can be dropped to the ground in a maul (converting a maul to a ruck) as long as the ball is placed away from the line of play, in other words back towards team-mates and away from the opposition (otherwise, of course, it would count as a forward pass or knock-on). The other significant distinguishing feature is that no player can touch the ball with their hand inside a ruck; only feet can be used until the ball reaches the back foot of the ruck, whereupon only that forward or the scrum-half can pick it up as described.

Rugby games are frequently spent with the forwards moving from maul to ruck to maul, and the backs may complain that they never get to see the ball, let alone run with it. Equally, the forwards will complain that when they do pass the ball to the backs, the latter promptly lose it to the opposition, and the forwards then have to go and get it back again.

New rules relating to rucks and mauls seem to come into effect from season to season, so do check with your player if you can't understand what's happening or check the World Rugby website at laws.worldrugby. org/ for the latest instructions. Also very helpful in giving the average person an idea of current thoughts on these aspects of playing rugby is

≫ www.rugby-sidestep-central.com.

Number 8s are obviously key players in the forward pack at all set piece plays. They decide whether to continue pushing forward in a ruck or whether to try to run the ball again and try to progress with another maul or ruck if they get tackled. At scrums, they use their feet to keep the ball inside the scrum so that the opposition pack have to remain bound together, and they stop the opposing scrum-half from touching the ball until it comes out from the scrum.

So it's quite important that the scrum-half and number 8 get on well – they spend an awful lot of the match standing very close to each other and making vital decisions on behalf of their team-mates. Because of their tactical skills and indeed their sheer size, number 8s are frequently appointed team captains, and they command respect from both forwards and backs in equal measure.

Infringements (various) to be avoided, including dangerous play

The high tackle

You can regularly hear rugby commentators on television point out the dubious value of the high tackle. It flattens the best player in the opposition and can prevent him from taking any further part in the game. It is, of course, completely illegal, and, thankfully all junior coaches and referees actively discourage its use, severely punishing any player who attempts it by removing them from the pitch – sometimes for the remainder of the game. Players have been banned from playing in the following game, or even longer, for dangerous high tackles.

A high tackle is one where the player grabs at their opponent's shoulders, neck or head, instead of grasping at their body around or below the waist. At junior level, tall players will complain that it is difficult to get down low enough to tackle smaller players, but all players must learn that a high tackle has the potential to be lethal.

Grabbing players by the collars of their shirts is similarly discouraged and will be penalised by a penalty kick being given to the opposition. Again in severe cases, the offender will be sent off the pitch. At senior level this can be for a 10 minute *sin bin* wait on the touch line, indicated by the referee showing a yellow card, but they can also be sent off, or red-carded, just like association football players. They take no further part in the game if the tackle is considered sufficiently dangerous.

The (accidental) forward pass

As you now know, all passes which do not go laterally or behind the ball carrier are called forward passes and are illegal in rugby. They result in the ball being handed to the opposition for a scrum. All players will tell you that such passes are accidental, and indeed for juniors, given their level of competence, this will actually probably be true.

The hand-off

This is a useful weapon in the armoury of the more experienced rugby players. It consists of running with the ball tucked under one arm whilst holding the other arm out to the side so that any unsuspecting opposition tackler will be pushed out of the way by the force of the oncoming player's hand and arm. This can be likened to jousting, where the lance was held out in front of the rider so that he could topple his opponent by galloping at speed towards him.

It is a perfectly legal way of resisting being tackled but only with a bent arm and to the side of the player. 'Jousting' as such is not legal. It has a great psychological effect on the opposition once it is perfected. The sight of a large forward (or even a back) charging at you with his arm outstretched is surely enough to put fear into the bravest of little souls. The thought of having your shoulder pummelled by this speeding ramrod must be terrifying when it is first encountered.

Of course, the hand-off should only ever be aimed at the opponent's body, never their face, and it is an important technique to learn to use with care. Those who attack the opposition above the shoulder can be accused of high tackles which will always result in a penalty being awarded, and they may get sent off.

Pulling down the scrum

Scrums can and do collapse. The group hug can rapidly turn into what seems to be a group orgy (frequently punctuated with loud shouts of 'watch where you're stamping' and 'mind my head'). Usually the collapse is unintentional, but occasionally it is deliberate.

This is, of course, a practice which should be severely discouraged from the earliest days, since it can result in very serious back and neck injuries to the forwards, and all players are taught that it is illegal. If a referee believes the scrum has been deliberately brought down, he will penalise the team involved by offering their opposition a penalty kick. The referee demonstrates this by a double victory salute with both arms bent and clenched fists towards him which he pulls down in a move similar to a dance move much beloved by bad-dancing dads.

All forwards should be taught that the aim of scrummaging is to push forwards against your opponents to push them up and back away from the ball and enable the ball to be heeled back to their own team's scrum-half. Once good practice has been absorbed, it will hopefully never be forgotten and less dangerous play will safeguard all players' future rugby careers.

The sport is very aware of the potential for injury and has extremely useful information on prevention on its website:

>> www.irbplayerwelfare.com/?documentid=52

Holding onto the ball

When tackled and brought down to the ground, the ball must be released immediately (either by passing it to team-mates whilst being tackled or by placing the ball onto the ground for the first player who reaches it to pick it up). If the ball is not released, the team is penalised with a penalty kick being given to the opposition. The referee can be seen apparently hugging himself to demonstrate that the offending player was holding onto the ball.

You will see tackled players holding the ball off the grass and squirming on the ground under their tacklers so they can turn their bodies away from the opposition to ensure they face their own team before placing the ball back onto the ground for one of them to pick up. If the ball touches the ground, it should be released immediately, and if it's not – that's holding onto the ball.

Offside

Rugby's offside law restricts where on the field players can be at any time to ensure there is space to attack and defend. A player is generally in an offside position if he is farther forward than the ball carrier or the team-mate who last played the ball. Whilst being in an offside position is not, in itself, an offence (much like football's offside law), any player who finds themselves offside should not take part in the game until they get themselves onside again. Of course, if they do touch the ball before moving back onside, they will be penalised.

Foul play in general

Any foul play should be discouraged, and the final lesson for all rugby players to learn is to control their tempers at all times – no matter how much they believe they have been provoked. If they can learn to control their own tempers, fewer injuries and penalties will occur. It's a good life lesson for them all.

The sin bin?

Advantage being played after an infringement

Sometimes in the course of a game an infringement occurs where a stoppage in play would deprive the team that did not offend of an opportunity to score. Under these circumstances, the Laws state that even though a team should be awarded a penalty, free kick or scrum, the players are given an opportunity to continue to play and attempt to score a try (assuming of course they retain control of the ball).

New supporters are frequently confused when an obvious infringement takes place, but play continues and then some time later the referee blows his whistle and takes the players back to the place where the first infringement happened for the penalty.

It can sometimes seem a very long time has elapsed between the original foul and the penalty being awarded, but if this happens, the referee will have been applying the Law of *advantage* to give the attacking team a chance to score. If they are unable to take advantage and attack, as long as only a relatively short period of time has elapsed, the referee can choose to return to the original infringement and award the penalty.

Supporters will see that initially during this advantage period the referee will hold his arm out to indicate he is playing advantage. Once his arm drops to his side or he calls out 'advantage over', the advantage period has ceased. However, with referees running hard to chase a game, holding their arm out sometimes gets forgotten and apparent ends to advantage prove unfounded when the referee still takes the players back to the scene of the first infringement even though he dropped his arm a few moments earlier.

Once advantage is truly over, whatever happens next, the team originally given the advantage with the ball will no longer get the penalty that might previously have been awarded. That penalty has timed out.

Teams playing advantage can therefore make risky moves in the full knowledge that if they don't work out, they will get to return to the site of the penalty and gain the advantage that way. For instance, this is the time when risky drop kicks at goal get taken. The lucky team is often able to take full advantage and score from such situations, so this Law can be very influential in the final result of a match.

Injuries and protective clothing

The leaders of the game are very aware of the potential for injury in this fast and furious contact sport, and we've already directed you to the World Rugby's detailed webpage. The Laws are regularly updated to ensure such injuries are kept to a minimum, but an occasional black eye will still occur (and indeed at junior level it is often worn with some pride by the owner).

Safety equipment has increased in the past decade, and as well as the traditional mouthguard (best obtained from your local dentist unless your child's club or school arranges special fitting sessions - see page 39 for more information), padded undershirts with soft shoulder pads are now worn at senior level. If a player is unfortunate enough to sustain an injury, it's always useful to know which local A&E department has the best reputation in these days of NHS cuts. Generally injuries will only be minor bumps and bruises, and a hot bath and ice pack will resolve most of these relatively rapidly. Special medical ice packs are available, but a bag of frozen peas wrapped in a tea towel will usually do the job cheaply and efficiently.

The importance of correct studs in playing boots will become very obvious the first time your child is stamped on or climbed over in a ruck or maul. With safety studs, the resultant marks will be relatively minor and will heal rapidly. This would not be the case with standard football studs.

We all know the value of cold steak on a black eye, but there are alternatives. A traditional remedy is an application of a tincture of arnica, surgical spirit and water, or another of vinegar and water, but our favourite is witch-hazel liquid or gel, both readily available from your local pharmacy – just don't apply it to open wounds because it will sting!

The following is an interesting combination recommended by Mrs Beeton of Household Management fame: 'chloride of ammonium (sal-ammoniac), 1 oz; rectified spirit, lavender water, or eau-de-Cologne, 2 oz; vinegar, 3 oz; water to make 16 ozs in all. Rags dipped in this solution should be laid over the bruise and kept constantly wet.' She notes that hot poultices are frequently more effective than cold applications in removing the associated discolouration. For this generation, a hot bath, an ice pack and some arnica and witch-hazel will usually do the trick. It is also easy now to buy oral arnica and arnica cream as treatments for bruising and shock from your local chemist or health food shop.

If your player gets cramps, we recommend magnesium capsules. Magnesium sulphate paste works well on splinters and any gravel or grit embedded in knees or hands. We could go on, but you get the idea; most wounds are minor and just require basic first aid. Hopefully your child or partner will never experience a serious injury.

The rugby lawmakers have also recently updated their rules on concussion. Although not frequent, concussions do occur when players land awkwardly from line-outs or after tackles are made. Full details of their recommendations can be found here:

>> www.irbplayerwelfare.com/concussion

In earlier times, a player would just be asked if he felt alright after being knocked out, sometimes being asked to count how many fingers the referee was holding in front of his face to check he was not still dizzy. If he seemed fine, he would continue to play, but this has all been updated to reflect modern medical knowledge, and players are removed from the pitch at any sign of concussion and frequently banned from playing again for a period until all signs of concussion have been checked and cleared. This revised attitude to incidents of concussion certainly reassures concerned parents that the game is doing everything it can to ensure player safety.

Learning how to lose gracefully

It is vital that all players learn that winning is not always possible, and losing gracefully is a skill that all good sportsmen and sportswomen should embrace. You can encourage your young player to do this by not getting too upset yourself when they lose. A supporter's role is more than patching up bodily injuries; boosting self-confidence and morale through encouragement is also part of your role in endorsing the spirit of good sportsmanship.

Rugby sevens

This version of rugby is generally played over seven minutes each way, rather than the 80 minutes of a full-side game, with just seven players on each side and three players per side in the scrum. Still under the Rugby Union banner, this version of the game uses the standard scoring system at senior level. Sevens is a faster, more try-friendly game with a shorter playing time and a tendency to have runaway results.

Sevens competitions at senior levels are also usually one- or two-day affairs. Schools play in sevens competitions, too, and these are often all-day events that can be great fun to support.

Competitions take place all over the world at senior level with teams arranged in groups; points are awarded for wins and draws with group winners moving on to the next stage of the competition.

You can find out more at

>> www.worldrugby.org/sevens-series/ and
>> www.rugbysevensguru.com/.

Rugby Tens also exists as a pre-season training game, with five forwards and five backs per team. Play is 10 minutes each way but includes full contact tackles. Pre-season Tens festivals now take place around the world, and this is another great way to get into enjoying rugby as the games are shorter but fast and furious and therefore great fun to watch.

Detailed laws exist for both these versions of the game:

>> Ten-a-side: laws.worldrugby.org/index.php?variation=3
>> Seven-a-side: laws.worldrugby.org/index.php?variation=2

Supporters' etiquette

If you've ever been taken aback by the behaviour of rowdy football crowds, keen rugby supporters – especially parents – can be just as vociferous and ill-mannered. All schools ask their supporters to behave correctly at matches, and some even issue their parents with guidelines, but this doesn't stop overly keen parents from screaming at their children mid-match, entreating them to 'kill' the opposition. Obviously this is not acceptable. Good supporters should cheer both sides, although a certain degree of bias can be shown, naturally.

Well-behaved supporters will encourage their team, whilst applauding good play by the opposition without antagonising the match officials. They will also shout for the whole team without embarrassing individuals by shouting out their names. Once supporters understand a bit more about the game, we can only hope they will not just stand in a huddle, nattering to each other, ignoring the match itself and getting cold, but will finally actually enjoy following the match properly with a keen interest in everything that's happening.

In England, those responsible for training young players are now guided by England Rugby's safeguarding policy:

» www.englandrugby.com/mm/Document/Governance/Safeguarding/ 01/30/56/33/RFUSafeguardingPolicyprinterfriendly_Neutral.pdf

Final thoughts

So there you have it. You know how many players are involved, what their positions and usual shirt numbers are, what is expected of them and how they play the game. You know pretty much everything you need to know to understand what's going on. You know the score in more ways than one.

Supporters are vitally important to the whole team, not just the individuals they come to watch. Cheers and encouragement make such a huge difference to the confidence of all the players and can make a struggling team overcome superior opposition. Do have faith in your team - you never know what they are capable of unless you cheer them on. Just listen to a Wales vs England match, and you'll hear the sounds of 'Swing Lo, Sweet Chariot' echoing around the stadium from the England fans and 'Cwm Rhondda' from the Welsh drowning them out.

And, of course, as you know, the supporters' role covers far more than valiant cheers from the touch line in all weathers - all the back-up work, kit preparation, safety equipment, the washing mountain, coping with injuries and defeats, helping with team teas … what would they do without you?

A simple glossary of terms

advantage
: A decision taken by the referee to allow players to continue to play after an infringement, if those holding the ball can gain an advantage by doing so.

All Blacks
: The New Zealand national men's rugby team – famous for their opening to every match, the Maori Haka (a war cry).

attack
: To move the ball forwards in order to score.

backs
: Numbers 9 to 15 of a team, the runners and tacklers in open play.

ball
: The oval ball designed to bounce obtusely to make life interesting for the receiving player. Balls come in four sizes:
Size 3 mini rugby age groups – Under 7, Under 8 and Under 9
Size 4 Junior rugby age groups – Under 10, Under 11, Under 12, Under 13 and Under 14
Size 4.5 Women's rugby / age groups – Under 15 and above, into senior rugby
Size 5 Full-sized rugby / age groups – Under 15 and above, into senior rugby

ball carrier
: The player holding the ball and running with it in his hands.

beach rugby
: An alternative to tag rugby, using similar rules, played with a size 4 ball on a beach, no shoes allowed and boys and girls can play together.

box kick
: A kick taken by the scrum-half when facing his own team (generally near a ruck, maul or scrum),

when he kicks the ball high up and back over his shoulder in the direction of the opposition to surprise them.

chip and chase	To give a short shallow kick over or around your opponent, then chase after it and hopefully gather it and continue to move forwards.
clearance kick	A kick taken during play to move the ball quickly down the pitch, sometimes a punt, sometimes a drop kick.
conversion	A kick for goal after scoring a try for two extra points on the scoreboard.
converted try	A combination of a try and a conversion scoring seven points.
core values	The RFU prides itself on its core values which include Teamwork, Respect, Enjoyment, Discipline and Sportsmanship – essential to keeping the game safe and enjoyable for all.
crossbar	The horizontal bar that connects the goalposts; conversion kicks and penalty field goals must go above this bar, not below it, to score points.
dangerous play	Any action that could injure another player.
dead ball line	The line behind the goalposts – not more than 22 metres from the try line.
drop goal (also *field goal*)	This is a drop kick through the goalposts and over the crossbar during normal play, scoring three points.
drop kick	A kick in which the ball is dropped to the ground before being struck with the foot.

drop out	A kick taken from the 22-metre line after the ball has gone dead behind the dead ball line.
field goal	See drop goal.
forwards	Numbers 1 to 8 in the team who compete for the ball at scrums and line-outs and carry and move the ball through mauls, rucks and open play.
forward pass	An illegal pass thrown to a position ahead of the player who threw it.
foul	An infringement of the laws; illegal play.
goal (1)	A successful kick between the goalposts and over the crossbar that earns two points for a conversion and three points for a penalty kick.
goal (2)	The H-shaped structures at each end of the pitch with two upright *goalposts* and a *crossbar*.
goal line (or *try line*)	The lines at each end of the pitch on which the goalposts are erected. See *try line* for more details.
goalposts	A rugby goal is shaped like the letter 'H', and the goalposts are the two vertical posts connected by a crossbar.
grubber kick	A short shallow kick past an opponent along the ground which will force the opposition to stop and turn. The defence may find it more difficult to collect or gather the ball from the ground, so keeping the ball low with a grubber kick will help.
half	A period of play lasting 40 minutes.
halfway line	A line across the pitch 50 metres from each try line.
hand off	A defensive technique involving the ball carrier pushing away the tackler with an open palmed hand,

illegal with a straight arm, the attacking player can only use a bent arm in this move.

high tackle	A dangerous tackle above the shoulder of the ball carrier.
IRB	International Rugby Board – the lead organisation for rugby around the world – now branded World Rugby.
kick-off	A drop kick to start a period of play at the start of each half or after a team has scored a try.
knock-on	A foul of knocking or dropping the ball forward onto the ground towards the opposition.
linesman/ lineswoman	An alternative name for the referee's assistants (*touch judges*) who run up and down the touch lines, one for each touch line, advising the referee on infringements and locations for line-outs.
line-out	A formation of two lines of forwards with a channel between them into which the ball is thrown to restart play after the ball goes into touch.
maul	A convergence of players around a ball carrier to push him and the ball forward with the ball OFF the ground.
mini rugby	A game played by young children with less contact than the full game.
obstruction	A foul of obstructing a player by blocking, tripping, shirt-pulling.
offside	Players standing ahead of the previous ball player in their own team are offside and are not allowed to touch the ball until they get back onside. If they do touch the ball, this is an illegal move which is penalised.

open play	Teams passing or kicking the ball from player to player across the pitch are playing in open play.
pack	The forwards are frequently referred to as 'the pack'.
pass	A legal throw of the ball to a team-mate.
penalty kick	A free kick awarded by the referee that can be used to kick for goal, or over the touch line to force a line-out, without possession being lost to the opposition.
penalty try	A try awarded by the referee when he feels that a foul or series of fouls have been deliberately committed to prevent a try being scored.
pitch	The playing field on which rugby is played. Most pitches are grass, though some have surfaces of clay, sand or even snow.
place kick	A kick taken by placing the ball on the pitch, stepping back and then moving in and kicking it. Before taking a place kick, some players use sand, a small hole dug into the pitch, a mound of earth or a plastic tee to position the ball.
punt	A kick in which the ball is dropped from the hand and kicked before it touches the ground. Often used in open play to gain ground. Also used when a penalty is awarded, to kick the ball into touch.
put-in	The action of the scrum-half placing the ball into the scrum.
red card	A card shown by the referee to a player being sent off the pitch for the rest of the game.
RFU	Rugby Football Union – the English management organisation.

ruck	A pack of linked players that forms over a ball to push the opposing team backwards and gain control of the ball. Rucks usually start after a tackle, but they can start whenever the ball is loose ON the ground.
Rugby League	The breakaway rugby code that was set up in 1895 to allow players to legally earn money from the game.
Rugby Sevens/Tens	The forms of Rugby Union with only seven or ten players per team, played over much shorter time-scales than the full team game.
Rugby Union	The rugby code that used to be for amateur players only, though now professionals can also play. The most popular form of rugby in the world today
scrum/ scrummage/ scrimmage	A set play for forwards during which the ball is contested for on the ground by the packs from both teams.
sending off	The red-card penalty for which a player must leave the pitch for the rest of the game.
sin bin	The area off the pitch where a player must wait for 10 minutes while serving a yellow card punishment, usually close to the team benches.
tackle	Action taken to stop a player from running with the ball. Ideally, tackles take place around and below the waistline. Above the shoulders they are illegal *high tackles*. Both players involved in the initial tackle must roll away from the ball once it is released to allow other players to access it.
tap tackle	A tackle made by tapping the back of the runner's legs or feet to upset his balance and cause him to trip up and fall to the ground where he must release the ball if he is held by a member of the opposition.

tag rugby	A version of the game for girls and boys, playing together or separately, and as a training system for older players. It involves wearing a tag belt that holds a 'tag' which counts as a tackle when it is removed from the wearer's belt.
throw-in	The action of the hooker throwing the ball over and between the two rows of forwards at a line-out.
touch	The area located outside the two touch lines on either side of the pitch. A ball is said to be *in touch* when it is in this area.
touch line	One of two lines that form the long sides of the playing area. The touch judges run along the touch lines and signal when the ball goes out. Supporters usually stand on the touch lines, too.
touch judge	The referees' assistant and the official who raises a flag if the ball goes into touch and indicates which side should be given the ball to throw in at a line-out.
touch rugby	A form of rugby in which players stop opponents from running with the ball by touching them lightly with a hand instead of tackling; used at junior level as a starting game and at senior level to increase handling skills.
try	The act of taking the ball over the try line and grounding it with downward pressure to earn five points.
try line/*goal line*	The line(s) at each end of the pitch on which the goalposts are erected, which is crossed in order for a try to be scored; a ball placed on the line will also count as a try.

tunnel

The gap between and below the front rows in a scrum into which the scrum-half puts the ball to restart a game after a stoppage.

veteran's rugby

A version of the game designed for older players, based on the standard 15-a-side game but with uncontested scrums and a recommendation that it should not be taken too seriously. Aggressive tackles are not welcomed.

wheeling the scrum

The act of deliberately moving the scrum round to put one team offside.

World Rugby

The new branding for the International Rugby Board (IRB), the organisation which oversees as all aspects of the game worldwide.

yellow card

The card shown by the referee to a player being cautioned for dangerous play which didn't result in an injury. A yellow card is also shown for a deliberate or 'professional' foul, committed to prevent a try being scored. The player is sent off the pitch for 10 minutes, to the *sin bin*.

XV

Latin for 15 – as in 1st XV team at school or club.

Want to learn more?

This reference list of websites will allow anyone interested in getting more involved in rugby the chance to explore it in more detail. We cannot take any responsibility for the accuracy of the links which may alter after publication, but hopefully most are long-lived websites that will continue for many years to come.

Main website:

The International Rugby Board
» www.worldrugby.org/

The IRB/World Rugby supplies full information on how to play, the Laws that govern the game, full training techniques and pretty much anything else you want to know about Rugby Union worldwide.

Other useful websites for information on rugby:

» www.rugbyfootballhistory.com

» www.englishclub.com/vocabulary/sports-rugby.htm

» www.englandrugby.com/my-rugby/coaches/new-rules-of-play/

» www.livestrong.com/sscat/rugby/

» www.activenewzealand.com/resources/rugby-rules.php

» www.teachpe.com/rugby/index.php

» superskyrockets.hubpages.com/hub/Rugby-League-vs-Rugby-Union

» en.wikipedia.org/wiki/Rugby_union

>> www.differencebetween.net/miscellaneous/differences-between-rugby-and-football/

>> www.schoolsrugby.co.uk/

>> www.bbc.co.uk/sport/0/rugby-union/

>> www.rbs6nations.com

>> www.planetrugby.co.uk/

>> www.rfu.com/ (England Rugby Union)

>> www.wru.co.uk/ (Welsh Rugby Union)

>> www.scottishrugby.org/

>> www.irishrugby.ie/

>> www.ffr.fr/ (French Rugby)

>> www.federugby.it/ (Italian Rugby)

>> www.rugby.com.au/ (Australian Rugby)

>> www.nzru.co.nz/ (New Zealand Rugby)

>> www.nzrugby.co.nz/ (New Zealand club & school rugby)

>> www.allblacks.com/

>> www.sarugby.net/ (South Africa Rugby and Springboks)

>> www.usarugby.org/

>> www.rugbycanada.ca/

>> www.uar.com.ar/ (Argentina Rugby)

This list is not exhaustive, and you can, of course, search the web for your local Rugby Union website, for national teams and other sides throughout Europe and worldwide, and for more information on your own team.

Kit suppliers

>> www.sportsdirect.com/rugby

>> www.genesissports.co.uk

>> www.kitbag.com/stores/kitbag/rugby.aspx

>> www.sportsworldrugby.co.uk

>> www.airosportswear.com/

>> www.viper10.com//rugby-kit-gallery

>> First XV - Rugbystuff.com

Notes

This year's team positions – complete in pencil to allow for reuse. We've allowed for up to eight players for multiple friends and family.

Name		Position	
Name		Position	
Name		Position	
Name		Position	
Name		Position	
Name		Position	
Name		Position	
Name		Position	
Rugby coach(es) this season:			
Points system for the current season (current score system 2015):			
Try (5 points)			
Conversion (2 points)			
Drop goal (3 points)			
Penalty kick (3 points)			

Game scores

Fixture versus & date	Home or away	School/ Club score	Opp. score	Our player's score	Comments
Example School 24.10.12	A	12	13	6 (2 pens.)	Good game – only two tries though and both scored by the opposition

This will be useful at the end of the season when team reports need to be handed in.

These will greatly endear your young player or partner to his team captain, who is frequently given the job of supplying such details to the sports teacher or team coach.

IF YOU'VE ENJOYED THIS BOOK, WHY NOT LOOK OUT FOR OUR OTHERS TITLES:

FOOTBALL *MADE SIMPLE*   Sept 2015

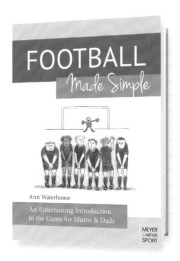

This book is dedicated to that hardy band of supporters who stand by the sides of pitches across the country in pouring rain, howling wind and whatever else the British weather can throw at them, watching groups of kids kicking a large, round and very muddy ball up and down a field, occasionally interrupted by someone with a whistle who stops the game, only to start it again shortly afterwards.

PLANNED PUBLICATION:

CRICKET *MADE SIMPLE*   April 2016

Credits

Text:	© Copyright 2015 Ann M Waterhouse
Illustrations:	© Copyright 2015 Amanda Stiby Harris
Cover Illustration:	© Copyright 2015 Amanda Stiby Harris
Copyediting:	Elizabeth Evans
Layout, Typesetting, Jacket & Cover:	Eva Feldmann

Notes